# Don't do that!

By Janine Amos and Annabel Spenceley
Consultant Rachael Underwood

A Cherrytree Book

Designed and produced
by A S Publishing

Copyright this edition © Evans Brothers Ltd 2003
First published in 1999
by Cherrytree Books
a division of the Evans Publishing Group
2A Portman Mansions
Chiltern St
London W1U 6NR

First published in paperback 2003. Reprinted 2004

*British Library Cataloguing in Publication Data*

Amos, Janine
   Don't do that!. – (Good friends)
   1.Friendship – Pictorial works – Juvenile literature
   I. Title II.Annabel Spenceley
   302.3'4

ISBN 1 84234 151 0

Printed and bound in Malaysia

# The new rabbit

Josh has a new rabbit. He shows Liam.
"He's called Bouncer," says Josh.

"Can I hold him?" asks Liam.
Josh nods.

Josh passes Bouncer to Liam.

Bouncer wriggles.
Liam squeezes him tight.

"Don't do that!" shouts Josh.
"You'll drop him!"

Josh tries to pull Bouncer back.
"Let go!" he says.

The rabbit is frightened.

Liam lets go of Bouncer.

"I only wanted to hold him," says Liam.
**How does Liam feel?**

"Squeezing hurts. You have to hold him
like this," says Josh.

Liam strokes Bouncer.

Then he holds him gently in his arms.

# Toothpaste

Sasha's in the bathroom.
She finds the toothpaste. It's red.

She makes a pattern on the bath.

She makes a pattern on the wall.

She makes a pattern all along the hallway.

In Mummy's bedroom,
Sasha paints the mirror.

Leanne sees Sasha.
She sees the mess.

23

"Don't do that!" shouts Leanne.

"Waah!" cries Sasha.

Mum rushes in.
"Look what she's done!" says Leanne.

Mum looks. She takes a deep breath.

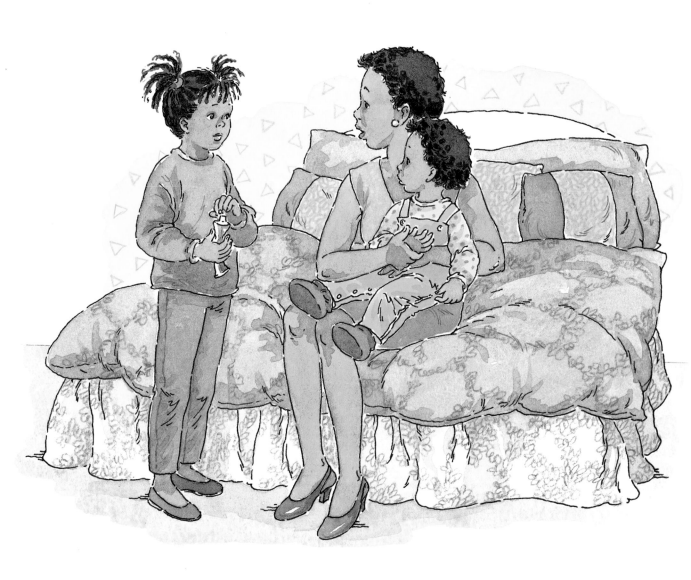

"Sasha doesn't know about toothpaste yet," says Mum.

"We need to show her what it's for."
Leanne gets her toothbrush.

"Look, Sasha. Toothpaste is for
teeth," says Leanne.

Sasha grabs the toothbrush and grins.
She has no teeth to clean.

If someone does something you don't like, it's important to tell them. Saying "Don't do that!" is one way of letting people know you don't like what they are doing.

It's even more helpful to tell them what you do want instead. Then they will know what you'd like them to do.